Introduction

There can be few people in the country who are not now aware of Pam Ayres' prowess as a poetess and entertainer. In something less than a year she has become almost an 'establishment' figure in the world of entertainment following her first appearing on *Opportunity Knocks*. On radio and television, and at numerous live concerts and recitals, her inimitable performances of her own work have endeared her to an enthusiastic audience of millions. Some of her most notable performances have been in the B.B.C. series *The Black and White Minstrel Show* in the spring where Pam featured as resident poetess. Then following the first programme in the successful new comedy series *What's On Next* (ITV, August 16th, 1976) Peter Knight, T.V. critic of the *Daily Telegraph* was moved to write:

> "Pam Ayres, who both writes and recites poetry, has some delicious fun revelling in the sheer atrociousness of some of her lines and also emerges as quite a comedienne. She has a completely natural sense of timing and that rare gift of being able to strike an instant rapport with her audience."

Her book *Some Of Me Poetry*, published in January, was an immediate success heading the paperback best-sellers list for many weeks and being in the top three for several months. Also her first L.P. which is virtually a reading (and singing!) of the book was one of the leaders in the L.P. charts for a long period.

To help satisfy the increasing popular demand for her work in printed form, this book *Some More Of Me Poetry* contains a further selection of delicious poems plus two songs, and by sheer coincidence a second L.P. is also being issued by Galaxy Records (see title page for details).

Pam does not intend to let these successes and the ensuing fame alter her life too much. She still lives in the depths of Oxfordshire although she has moved from the small flat in Witney to a small house.

Now, surrounded by cornfields, she can devote her time to thinking, and writing more of the poems that we enjoy so much.

September 1976   R.G.E.

The Spot Welder's Dream

I wish I was a pop star,
Colourful and brash,
With me earoles full of crochets,
And me wallet full of cash,
To hide me bit of acne,
I'll stick sequins on me face,
Then I can do the vocals,
And you can do the base.
Yeah.

I can do the vocals,
But to whip them to a frenzy,
Seated at the Organ,
We'll have rockin' Bert McKenzie,
Now Bert's a lovely mover,
But he tends to be a dunce,
When he's winking at the boppers,
He shuts both eyes at once.

SOME MORE OF ME POETRY

Pam Ayres

Introduced and Illustrated by Roy Garnham Elmore

Published by:

GALAXY RECORDS
223 Regent Street
London W1R 8TD

Telephone 01-734 9768

The NEW Pam Ayres L.P.
"Pam Ayres, Vol. II—Some More Of Me Poetry" GAL 6010,
and her first L.P. "Pam Ayres, Vol. I" GAL 6003
are now available from Galaxy Records.

These are also available on Cassette
GALC 6003 (Vol. I) and GALC 6010 (Vol. II).

ISBN 0.9504774.1.9

Contents:

I'll buy a cossack shirt,
Split to the waist, in peacock red,
So me face will get them going,
And me chest will knock them dead,
I'll wave me great long legs about,
And wrap them round the mike,
I had a practice Saturday,
But I fell off me bike.

I'll get meself an agent,
And a manager and all,
A bloke to drive the minibus,
And one to book the hall,
A musical arranger,
And a private record plugger,
So when we're in the charts,
Well, we shall all feel that much smugger.

And when we're doing a stand,
I'll come up quiet, to the mike,
I'll stick me pelvis out,
And say "Right on . . ." suggestive like,
I'll drive the women crazy,
They'll be in such a state,
And they'll scratch each other's eyes out,
Once I've had me teeth put straight.

Farewell Cradley Heath!
We're out upon the road to fame,
Farewell factory gates!
We're going to be a Household Name,
Good riddance Welding Shop,
And factory hooter every morn,
For it's me and Bert McKenzie,
A Superstar is born.

I am a Cunning Vending Machine

I am a cunnin' vending machine,
Lurkin' in the hall,
So you can't kick me delicate parts,
I'm bolted to the wall,
Come on! Drop in your money,
Don't let's hang about,
I'll do my level best to see,
You don't get nothing out.

I sees you all approachin'
The fagless and the dry,
All fumblin' in your pockets,
And expectant in the eye,
I might be in your place of work,
Or on the High Street wall,
Trust in me! In theory,
I cater for you all.

Within these windows I provide,
For every human state,
Hunger, night starvation,
And remembering birthdays late,
Just read the information,
Pop the money in—that's grand,
And I'll see absolutely nothing,
Ever drops down in your hand.

I might be at your swimming bath,
And you'd come, cold and wet,
With a shilling in your hand,
Some hot soup for to get,
And as you stand in wet
Anticipation of a sup,
I will dispense the soup,
But I will not dispense the cup.

And then it's all-out war,
Because you lost your half-a-nicker,
Mighty kicks and blows with bricks,
Will make me neon flicker,
But if you bash me up,
So I'm removed, me pipes run dry,
There's no way you can win,
I'll send me brother by and by.

Once there was friendly ladies,
Years and years before,
Who stood with giant teapots,
Saying "What can I do you for?"
They'd hand you all the proper change,
And pour your cup of tea,
But they're not economic so . . .
Hard Luck! You're stuck with me.

I am a...

I am a Witney Blanket,
Original and Best,
You'll never get cold feet,
With me across your chest.

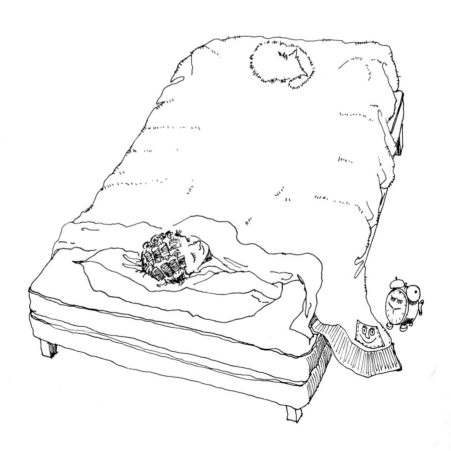

I am a...

I am a Dry Stone Waller,
All day I Dry Stone Wall,
Of all appalling callings,
Dry Stone Walling's,
Worst of all.

Little Lawrence Greenaway

Little Lawrence Greenaway,
He tended to digress,
He'd always tell you rather more,
Instead of rather less,
Of wild exaggeration
He was never known to tire,
The facts became irrelevant,
In short, he was a liar.

He said "I'm in computers,
You name the sort, we've gottem"
Whereas in fact he only
Screwed the castors on the bottom,
His claims they grew preposterous,
He couldn't understand,
Why all of his companions,
Well, they laughed, behind their hands.

One awful Monday morning,
He was sitting on the train,
He saw a great red-headed man,
Come rushing down the lane,
Just as the train was leaving,
The man wrenched at the door,
And stood above the passengers,
A mighty six foot four.

He opened up his great big mouth,
And with a ghastly shout,
Hollered "Somewhere on this train's
The bloke who took my Missis out!"
Lawrence he was frightened,
Like a frightened little rabbit,
But he still said "It was me"
You see, just through force of habit.

The great big man, he picked him up,
Underneath the throat,
And helped him off the train,
Without returning for his coat,
With his head locked in a headlock,
He was rushed off down the lane,
And little Lawrence Greenaway,
He were *never seen again.*

Walk with Me
For a Perch and a Rood

I don't want metrication, friends,
The milligramme and litre,
I work in feet and inches,
I do not trust the metre,
I cannot calculate it,
I don't know where I am,
Give me half a hundredweight,
And you can have a gramme.

Metrication? I can't learn it,
I am too long in the tooth,
My schooldays they are over,
Gorn! with the bloom of youth,
I work in tenths of inches,
The furlong and the chain,
The rood and pole, the six-foot hole,
I like it nice and plain.

I like it by the furlong,
And I like it by the acre,
I liked the bakers dozen,
And I also liked the baker,
I liked the bushel basket,
And a peck's alright by me,
Them metrics put the prices up,
As far as I can see.

I didn't want the decimals,
I don't want metrication,
I wouldn't know a litre,
If you poured it in a basin,
I'll have my pints and gallons,
As long as I am able,
My glass I'll fill with a sixth of a gill,
And I'll see you under the table!

The Dolly
on the Dustcart

I'm the dolly on the dustcart,
I can see you're not impressed,
I'm fixed above the driver's cab,
With wire across me chest,
The dustman see, he spotted me,
Going in the grinder,
And he fixed me on the lorry,
I dunno if that was kinder.

This used to be a lovely dress,
In pink and pretty shades,
But it's torn now, being on the cart,
And black as the ace of spades,
There's dirt all round me face,
And all across me rosy cheeks,
Well, I've had me head thrown back,
But we ain't had no rain for weeks.

I used to be a "Mama" doll,
Tipped forward, I'd say "Mum"
But the rain got in me squeaker,
And now I been struck dumb,
I had two lovely blue eyes,
But out in the wind and weather,
One's sunk back in me head like,
And one's gone altogether.

I'm not a soft, flesh coloured dolly,
Modern children like so much,
I'm one of those hard old dollies,
What are very cold to touch,
Modern dolly's underwear,
Leaves me a bit nonplussed,
I haven't got a bra,
But then I haven't got a bust!

Yet I was happy in that dolls house,
I was happy as a Queen,
I never knew that Tiny Tears,
Was coming on the scene,
I heard of dolls with hair that grew,
And I was quite enthralled,
Until I realised *my* head
Was hard and pink . . . and bald.

So I travels with the rubbish,
Out of fashion, out of style,
Out of me environment,
For mile after mile,
No longer prized . . . dustbinized!
Unfeminine, Untidy,
I'm the dolly on the dustcart.
There'll be no collection Friday.

Where There's a Will

...there's a sobbing relation.

All the family was gathered,
To hear poor Grandad's will,
Fred was watching Alice,
And she was watching Bill,
He was watching Arthur,
Everywhere he went,
But specially at the cupboard,
Where Grandad kept the rent.

Outside on the patio,
The sliding door was closed,
And sitting in a chair,
Was nephew John, his face composed,
He said "Me dear old Grandad,
I shall never see you more"
And his sheets of calculations,
Were spread across the floor.

Downstairs in the kitchen,
Sister Alice blew her nose,
Saying "He always was my favourite,
You *knew* that I suppose?
You couldn't have found a nicer man,
I've never loved one dearer,
I'd have come round *much* more often,
If I'd lived just that bit nearer."

Cousin Arthur sat alone,
His eyes were wild and rash,
And desperately he tried to think,
Where old folks hid their cash,
He'd thought about the armchair,
And the mattress on the bed,
And he'd left his car at home,
And booked a Pickfords van instead.

Then there were the bedroom floorboards,
He'd studied every crack,
And twice, while dusting the commode,
He'd rolled the carpet back,
But he knew the others watched him,
"You scavengers" he cursed,
And every night he prayed,
"Don't let the others find it first".

The day that Grandads' will was read,
It came up bright and clear,
The solicitor looked round,
And said, "Now then, are we all here?"
Someone shouted "Yes"
And someone else unscrewed his pen,
And someone sat upon his coat,
So he could not stand up again.

He carefully unfolded it
And wonderingly said,
"This is the shortest will,
I ever will have read,"
He rolled a fag and carefully,
Laid in a filter tip,
While beads of sweat they gathered,
On Cousin Arthur's lip.

It says: "Me dear relations,
Thank you all for being so kind,
And out beside the lily pond,
You will surely find,
The half a million pounds,
With which I stuffed me garden gnome,
Which I leave, with great affection,
To the Battersea Dogs Home."

All about Pumpkins

*In this part of Oxfordshire, pumpkin growing competitions are very popular.
In the spring, all contestants receive a seed from the same pumpkin. The heaviest
pumpkin from the plants reared is the winner. For one such Weigh-In, a tense
occasion at Bampton, I was asked to present the prize and come up with a
suitable poem. Here it is.*

I've been asked here this evening,
To congratulate the winner,
And also to encourage both,
The novice and beginner.
If your pumpkins are a problem,
And you never win a prize,
A little of the following,
Is what I would advise.

When you get your pumpkin seed
Don't drop it in the ground,
First, make sure that it is oval,
It's a tater if it's round,
And if your neighbour accidently,
Drops his by your shoe,
Make good and sure you stamp on it,
Then say it wasn't you.

Don't do the seed with Derris,
Or any fancy stuff,
Take it from your pocket,
Dusting off the bits of fluff,
And wait until its dark,
Before you go to bury it,
So no saboteur can come,
And shower it with Flit.

And when you are a-digging,
And turning of the sod,
Watch out where you put your boots,
Or on it you have trod,
Don't put a bucket over,
To make it long and white,
For when you take the bucket off,
It will fall down with fright.

But if the worst should happen,
And nextdoor's makes yours look small,
Here's your course of action,
'Cause that won't do at all,
You *could* bash theirs with a mallet,
But they'd suspect at once,
You've got to do it cunning,
It makes all the differ unce.

You takes hold of your pumpkin,
And this is cheating but,
The circumstance demands it,
And you makes a little cut,
Somewhere in the pumpkin,
In the front or in the back,
And you takes a great big lump of lead,
And stuffs it in the crack.

So when they put it on the scales,
Right before your eyes,
The needle will go whizzing round,
And you will win the prize,
Ignore the shouts of "Crooked!"
And scorn the cries of "Bent!"
Lead lining in your pumpkin,
Lends weight, to your argument.

Puddings — A SLICE OF NOSTALGIA

Don't open no more tins of Irish Stew, Alice,
You know it makes me pace the bedroom floor,
You gave me Irish Stew a week last Sunday,
And I never got to sleep till half past four,
You open up another tin of spam, Alice,
Or them frankfurter sausages in brine,
And we'll stab them, sitting opposite each other,
And you can dream your dreams, and I'll dream mine.

I'll dream about me apple cheeked old mother,
Her smiling face above a pot of broth,
She used to cook us every kind of pudding,
Proper puddings . . . in a pudding cloth!
When we came home from school all cold and hungry.
One look along the clothes line was enough,
And if the pudding cloth was there a-flapping,
We all knew what it meant—a suet duff!

A suet duff would set your cheeks a-glowing,
Suet duff and custard, in a mound,
And even if you'd run about all morning,
A suet duff would stick you to the ground,
Or else there'd be a lovely batter pudding,
With all the edges baked so hard and black,
So if your teeth had grown a bit too long like,
Well, that would be the stuff to grind them back.

She used to make us lovely apple puddings,
She'd boil them all the morning on the stove,
If you bit on something hard that wasn't apple,
The chances were, you'd bitten on a clove,
Or else there'd be a great jam roly poly,
We'd watch it going underneath the knife,
And if you took a bite a bit too early,
The red hot jam would scar your mouth for life.

Oh bring back the roly poly pudding,
Bread and butter pudding . . . Spotted Dick!
Great big jugs full up of yellow custard,
That's the sort of pudding I would pick,
But here's the tube of artificial cream, Alice,
I've cleaned the nozzle out, the hole's so fine,
And we'll squirt it on our little pots of yoghurt,
And you can dream your dreams, and I'll dream mine.

21

The Sea Shell

Don't ee fret no more, my darlin' Alice,
Don't ee cry and sorrow, my old dear,
Don't ee watch the lane for our son Arnold,
Lost upon the sea this fourteen year,
Let a smile play on your lips again, Alice,
Fourteen years, you've worn the widows drab,
And get your ear away from that great sea shell,
Nobody hears the ocean in a crab.

How I Loved You, Ethel Preedy, with Your Neck so Long and Slender

How I loved you, Ethel Preedy,
With your neck so long and slender,
At the Tennis Dance,
What magic charm did you engender!
Our eyes met in the crowd,
Your fingers tightened on the racquet,
But when I tore my gaze away,
Some swine had pinched me jacket.

The Baby Shop

There is a Baby Shop, at the corner of the street,
Where all sorts of people, coincidently meet,
Some who cannot do it, and some who've lost the knack,
And those who do not want to, and them with a Bad Back.

But you can buy a baby there of any shape or size,
They do them up with blue or green or brown or hazel eyes,
So you can choose whatever sort it is your wish to rear,
But if you want a clever one, they run a bit more dear.

They also have some special ones that don't look quite so nice,
But they can write the Lord's Prayer all on a grain of rice,
Or, if you are extremely rich, a Genius in Bud!
Guaranteed to think all day, and not play in the mud.

And if there is a local dialect you have to meet,
You can select a baby which will either cry or Greet,
And if you do not want a child who might appear coarse,
Choose one from "Pass the Ketchup" and not from "Gis the sourse"

The shop lays down requirements which you will have to meet,
To keep the baby safe and give him what he likes to eat,
They'll reject your application if you are a person what'll,
Holler at the baby and not sterilize his bottle.

But if you are admissible, then rush down to the Sales,
Pick one up at half the price and slap him on the scales,
After Bottle Break when they're contented and replete,
At the Baby Shop, at the corner of the street.

I fell for a
Black and White Minstrel

I fell for a black and white minstrel,
He tickled me under the chin,
What I wanted to say was "You go away"
But I actually said "Oh . . . come in"
In a minute I was captivated,
I had not a second to think,
What I could not erase, as I gazed in his face,
Was "What does he look like . . . pink!"

We went to his lodgings in Clapham,
Ostensibly we went for tea,
Only I kept on sort of looking at him,
And he kept sort of looking at me,
And the thing with a black and white minstrel,
They're not like a man who is clean,
If you've covered your chest, with a pearly white vest,
You can very soon see where he's been.

He sang me "Oh dem Golden Slippers!"
He danced me a pulsatin' dance,
With his muscular thighs, and his white-circled eyes,
A maiden like me stood no chance,
He flung off his gold lamé jacket,
And likewise his silver top hat,
He cared not a fig, as he tore off his wig,
And I'm telling you no more than that.

But too early the traffic grew louder,
And I knew that it had to be dawn,
I reached for me black and white minstrel,
But me black and white minstrel had gorn,
I sat all alone in the morning,
Not wanting to understand,
That I had been only a plaything,
I was only a pawn . . . in his hand.

To this day I still cherish the pillow,
Where my black and white minstrel did lie,
There was one little place, where he laid his black face,
And one where he laid his white eye,
Me black and white minstrel has left me,
Gorn! with never Goodbye,
But my heart will be with him in Clapham,
Till the waters of Swannee, run dry.

The Husband's Lament

or Well, You Certainly Proved Them Wrong.

The flowers round our garden gate,
Are strangled now with nettles,
The caterpillars got the leaves,
The road dust got the petals,
There's cracks across the asphalt path,
And the dusty wind do blow,
I know they say "domestic bliss"
But I dunno . . .

There's trikes chucked on the garden,
And there's writing on the wall,
The kids have smashed the wash house,
With their little rubber ball,
The paint's peeled off the woodwork,
And the gutter's sagging fast,
I bodged it up last Autumn,
But . . . it didn't last.

And in our shattered living room,
The telly's on the blink,
There's fag ends in the saucers,
And peelings in the sink,
There's holes burned in the carpet,
Where it smouldered half the night,
"A Woman's Work is Never Done"
And you certainly proved that right.

There's barnacles in the goldfish bowl,
And curlers on the floor,
The budgie's out the window,
And the woodworm's in the door,
The leaves fell off the rubber plant,
The leg fell off the bed,
The smiles fell off our faces,
And the back fell off the shed.

And *you*, who I adored,
One look and I knew I was falling,
You stole away my heart,
Beneath the moon and that tarpaulin,
It *can't* be you beside me,
With your tights so full of holes,
Chewing through your supper,
All them picalilli rolls.

We've been together twenty years today,
And there's a moral,
Since we have no conversation,
We have never had a quarrel,
We hardly see each other,
So we never have a fight,
For "Silence it is Golden"
And we've certainly proved that right.

Thank You
and Goodnight
All You Winklepickers

I hate this buying shoes,
I do, I hate it with a passion,
Whatever else I wear,
Me shoes are always out of fashion,
And that's because my feet,
Are everything I'd wish they're not,
They're long and wide and knobbly,
And usually they're hot.

Oh curse them winklepickers!
All turned up at the ends,
That I used to cram me feet in,
To go dancing with my friends,
I'd cut the light fantastic,
With a face so grim and sour,
And when I took them off,
I'd sit and laugh for half an hour.

Who *invented* winklepickers?
It's his fault that nowadays,
When I stroll along,
Me feet are pointing different ways,
I read that Chinese ladies,
Bound their feet up to the knees,
And they're welcome, if they like,
But then they're clever, these Chinese.

Whatever else I might be,
Indecisive I am not,
It's wellies when it's raining,
And plimsolls when it's hot,
I'm not saying that I have no shoes,
That statement would be wrong,
It's just I have to find one,
That's as broad as it is long.

When I shop for shoes,
I come up flapping in me daps,
And they show me little shoes,
With just a tracery of straps,
And as I stuff me foot in,
And the leather starts to crack,
I see the place is empty,
'Cause they're laughing round the back.

In the hope of dainty footwear,
I'll continue with the hunt,
Breathtaking in me slippers,
With the pom pom on the front,
And the one thing on my mind,
As I go flapping down the street,
Is why don't I entitle this:
I Wish I'd Looked After Me Feet.

The Flit Gun

My Mother had a Flit Gun,
It was not devoid of charm,
A bit of Flit,
Shot out of it,
The rest shot up her arm.

The Wedding

or..Was it Really you Round the Back of the Institute?

Come sit beside me love, now that the lamps are burning low,
We'll gaze upon our wedding cake lit softly in the glow,
Oh, it was a lovely one, with candles burning bright,
Not too hard or crumbly, Oh the texture was just right,
The icing was a masterpiece, the marzipan was soft,
The effigy of you and me both standing up aloft,
Don't hesitate to take some if I've tempted you enough,
It's marvellous. And someone ought to eat the bloody stuff.

And draped along the sofa is my lovely wedding gown,
Rented for a tenner from the other side of town,
With graceful sleeves of satin and the collar edged with lace,
Skilfully designed to softly frame my smilin' face,
With lovely sprigs of blossom where the cuff laid on my hand,
Which I had shyly offered to accept the wedding band,
The stately train which swept the aisle and floated all about,
To hopefully conceal the fact that I am growing stout.

And stuffed there in a jam jar, my unblemished brides bouquet,
With lovely ferns and lilies that entwine and fall away,
From scented stephanotis and a shy and rambling rose,
Set among the tendrils and the pastel satin bows,
I clutched it to my bosom as my love and I were wed,
That over my abdomen all the fronds should softly spread,
For though I knew, the frontal view, was just a blushing bride,
My shape I fear, did not appear, too hot viewed from the side.

And you, my love, with whom I shall withstand life's stormy weather,
Despite the fact we haven't got two pence to rub together,
Smile up at me from where you are prostrate upon the floor,
Still groggy from the stag night you arranged the night before,
And smile on us, Good Fortune, may our mighty mortgage shrink,
Keep us off Security, the panel and the drink,
Keep my stranglehold full on the gizzard of the purse,
As we travel on life's journey—for better or for worse.

The Vegetable Garden
and the
Runaway
Horse

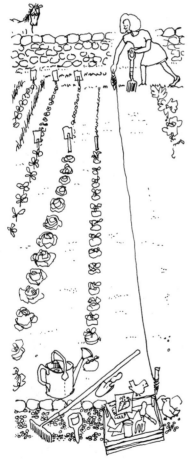

In everybody's garden now,
The grass has started growing,
Gardeners, they are gardening,
And mowers, . . . they are mowing,
Compost heaps are rotting down,
And bonfires burning low,
So I took up me shovel,
And resolved to have a go.

I dug a patch of garden,
That was not too hot or shady,
And not too large to tax
The constitution of a lady,
Everything which crossed my spade,
I flung it all asunder,
And that which I could not dig up,
I rapidly dug under.

And in my little plot,
I bravely laboured with the hoe,
Enthusiasm running rife,
I sprinted to and fro,
I stopped for nothing,
Not for food or drink or idle words,
Except a spotted dick,
Someone had chucked out for the birds.

Imagine then my pleasure,
As it all came sprouting out,
I cast aside me dibber,
And I swaggered round about,
But Alas, the gate,
To which my garden was adjacent,
Was open, and I never saw,
As up the path I hastent*

sorry folks

When I went down on Saturday,
A horse stood in my plot,
But nothing else stood in it,
For he'd eaten all the lot,
I said "Alas, my efforts wasted,
And my garden wrecked,
Go away, you rotten horse,"
(Or words to that effect.)

His hooves had crushed me lettuce,
And me radishes were mangled,
Broken canes were scattered,
Where me runner beans had dangled,
The lovely shiny marrow,
I'd been going to stuff and all,
The horse had broke it off it's stalk,
and kicked it up the wall.

Standing in the ruins,
Of me brussels sprouts and spinach,
I threw away me shovel,
And I said, "Well, thats the finich,
No early peas for me,
The birds can have them,
Or the mice might,
And if I want a cabbage,
Well, I'll see you down at Pricerite!"

The Annual Holiday

or Will that Old Army Suitcase Hold out Another Year Dad?

Well, I'm off on me holidays,
It's all within me reach,
I've got myself in trim,
For carting deckchairs round the beach,
With me flask of tea and cup,
I shall be pouring out the dregs,
With wasps all round me orange,
And with tar all round me legs.

All bundled up with cardigans,
(The weather's on the change)
I won't have slept the night before,
(The beds were all so strange)
I'll lay out on the beach,
Oh so remote and deeply tanned,
With me sandwiches, me knickers,
And me ears full up with sand.

At night, as we're on holiday,
It's on the town we'll go,
With sausage, chips and marrowfats,
At a couple of quid a throw,
And when we've spent our cash,
We'll wander home as best we can,
All along the Mini Golf,
To the smell of the hot dog man.

Or seeing as it's raining,
We'll pop out for a jar,
When we've fought the other tourists,
For a second at the bar,
We'll ignore those folks who've just come in,
Whose shoulders are so sore,
'Cause *last* week was so hot,
They couldn't step outside the door.

And then we'll travel home,
All sat religiously apart,
So we don't touch each others legs,
And make the sunburn smart,
With suitcasefuls of rock,
So everybody gets a stick,
And our hearts down in our flip flops,
See you next year. Kiss me quick.

Foolish Brother Luke

This poem is worthy of inclusion, if only for the fact that it was the first I ever wrote. It was for a Poetry Competition. Unfortunately the deadline for entries reached me before I could reach a more subtle ending!

Here it is . . .

And as the cock crew, brave undaunted sound,
Rocks, from off his head, were seen to bound,
And at the hour of dawn by luck or fluke,
Arose the form of Foolish Brother Luke.

Now Foolish Brother Luke, he had no sense,
He never listened to his good parents,
But places rough and low would oft frequent,
On alcohol and sordid pleasure bent.

One day Alas, he met his Waterloo,
For Luke he had no sense like me or you,
There he sat upon his own dustbin,
Eatin' a banana, in its' skin.

Sittin' on a bin across the road,
There lounged the form of Schemin' Annie Toad,
She knew he had some money, cause she'd seen,
Him in the dirty places, where he'd been.

Pattin' all her curlers into place,
And rubbin' cochineal upon her face,
She crossed the road to Luke and said "How do,
Foolish Brother Luke, I fancy you."

He choked on his banana, and he fell,
From off his bin a-cryin' "Bloody Hell!"
"At last it's happened, like I knew it would,
Come inside and have some . . . Christmas Pud!"

For Foolish Brother Luke was not so soft,
He'd pondered long up in his bedroom loft,
He knew *she* had some money, cause he'd seen,
Her, in the dirty places where she'd been.

But what Luke did not know, poor foolish lad,
Annie Toad was mistress to his Dad,
What Annie did not know, by luck or fluke,
Was that her Mum was not averse to Luke.

Annie Toad had blackmailed poor Luke's Dad,
To name her in his will and so he had,
But Luke to Annie's Mum had done the same,
So who, or why, or what was there to blame?

And so they wed, the gay misguided pair,
Throwin' all their money in the air,
But yet, a word of warnin' needed here,
They were struck by lightning.

The Secretary's Song

Secretary is my trade,
Shorthand typist, second grade,
With me pad clutched in me hand a
Living breathing memoranda,
Like a ramrod on the seat,
I will·sit up straight and neat,
With me feet placed close together,
I'll remark upon the weather,
But don't ask me more than that,
Because I haven't got the brain,
To respond.

I find when seated in my chair,
With my conscientious stare,
Stabbing pains come in me eye for
What you write, I can't decipher,
But when I rush in with the teas,
I'll charm the birds right off the trees,
I'll run to do the washing up
And pick the fag ends out the cup,
Until I hear the siren blow,
Then I'll just clock my card and go
Home.

I will not appear to choke,
In conferences thick with smoke,
In vain I'll write the boring minute,
And assume some interest in it,
I won't elaborate the facts,
And I won't come to work in slacks,
For they offend the royal eyeball,
And that cannot be allowed at all,
For what's the point of women
If you cannot see their legs?

And when at last I'm seated by,
The great typewriter in the sky,
Let me type the letters right,
In the morning and at night,
Let the Snopake grow on trees,
Let men's hands stay off me knees,
Let it be a place harmonic,
With no need for gin and tonic,
Thank you in anticipation
Of your favourable reply,
Craving your indulgence,
Yours sincerely.
Goodbye.

Oh Don't Sell our Edgar no more Violins

Oh don't sell our Edgar no more violins,
That dear little laddie of mine,
Though he's but eight, we'd prefer him to wait,
Or I doubt if he'll live to be nine,
He plays the same song, and it's sad, and it's long,
And when Edgar reaches the end,
With his face full of woe, he just rosins the bow,
And starts it all over again.

Now Daddy says Edgar's a right little gem,
It's only Daddy's *face* that looks bored,
It's really delight, makes his face appear white,
When Edgar scrapes out that first chord,
Daddy of course, he was filled with remorse,
When Edgar came home from the choir,
To find that his fiddle, well, the sides and the middle,
Were stuffed down the back of the fire.

So don't sell our Edgar no more violins,
When next he appears in your shop,
His Daddy and me, we are forced to agree,
His fiddlin' will soon have to stop,
Sell him a clean, or a filthy magazine,
Ply him with whisky or gin,
A teddy! A bunny! or just pinch the kids money,
But don't sell our Edgar no more violins.

For though it be a mortal sin,
We'll do the little fiddler in,
Don't sell our Edgar no more violins.

THE SECRETARY'S SONG

With resignation:

Se-cre—ta—ry is my trade Short-hand
ty-pist se-cond grade With me pad clutch'd in me
hand a Liv-ing breathing memor—an-da —— Like a
ram-rod on the seat I will sit up straight and
neat With me feet placed close together I'll remark upon the
wea—ther —— But don't ask me more than that B'cause I
hav-en't got the brain ———— To re - spond. ——

OH DON'T SELL OUR EDGAR NO MORE VIOLINS

With quiet desperation:

Oh don't sell our Ed-gar no more vi-o-lins That dear lit-tle lad-die of mine — Tho' he's but eight we'd pre-fer him to wait —— Or I doubt if he'll live —— to be nine —— He plays the same song —— and it's sad —— and it's long — And when Ed-gar reach-es the end —— With his face full of woe he just ro—sins the bow —— And starts it all o—ver—a— —gain.

Printed in England